101
WESTERN PLEASURE AND HORSEMANSHIP TIPS

101 Basics of Western Riding and Showing
WESTERN PLEASURE AND HORSEMANSHIP TIPS

Moira C. Harris

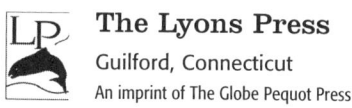

The Lyons Press
Guilford, Connecticut
An imprint of The Globe Pequot Press

Copyright © 2007 by Morris Book Publishing, LLC

The Lyons Press is an imprint of The Globe Pequot Press.

10 9 8 7 6 5 4 3 2 1

Printed in the United States of America

Designed by Sheryl P. Kober

ISBN 978-1-59228-861-8

Library of Congress Cataloging-in-Publication Data is available on file.

Contents

Acknowledgments

Special thanks go to Matt Rayl and Serrano Creek Ranch, Lake Forest, Calif., for allowing me to run amok on property; Leslie Thomson of Leslie Thompson Training, Lake Forest, Calif., for her wonderful assistance in organizing the troops; and the riders of Serrano Creek who gave their time and effort for the photographs in this book:

Brown Jaynes and Excaliber Ligero (King)
Alliston Statz and Dusty Jaguar (Jack)
Brianna Leahy and Gotta Invest (Rosie), owned by Joan Thomas
Karen Mundwiler and My Lady Joe Holly (Holly)
Jessie Hagadom and Blossom
Kassidy Harvey and Zippin By Me
Danielle Dollar and Reiner
Estelle Guerineau and Sis
Marc Hedgpeth and Jake Reynolds

And the biggest thank you to fellow author, editor, and friend Micaela Myers, my enthusiastic all-star cheerleader.

Introduction

There are plenty of books on Western riding. The catch is finding one that has the information that you really desire. Some Western books on competing also have big sections on cattle events, while others go in-depth about the finer points of colt starting. There are some very excellent titles that take the reader step by step into Western training—which is fine if the advanced elements of riding and training are understood, whereupon the reader can then go on and start, say, a futurity prospect.

But chances are that you're still seeking information on the fundamentals. You're not looking for information on "How to train my next World Show prospect," but rather "How do I get my horse to do what I want? How do I ride correctly on my horse?"

These words—your horse—are key in this book. These tips were gathered and assembled with the understanding that you indeed have a horse in your life: It may be the one grazing in your pasture, boarded at the local stable, or a horse that your friend lets you ride. You want to gain greater understanding about how to ride and handle this specific horse, not a nameless, faceless horse of the future, or some ideal of what you "should seek out and buy." Let's face it—we ride the horse that we have, and what we're really after is whatever information will make that relationship better. So this book is going to help you enjoy the horse you have now by giving you great Western horsemanship and riding tips that will assist you, whether that's ironing out the rough spots, or having a harmonious relationship overall.

As Joe Friday on Dragnet used to say, "Just the facts, ma'am," and that's what this book intends to give you: simple tips to help improve your riding and horsemanship, so you can enjoy your favorite pastime. And if you're looking to set a hoof in the show pen, there's plenty of good advice here that can help you have a winning ride. True, *101 Western Pleasure and Horsemanship Tips* won't help learn how to do a sliding stop with your next reining prospect, but it will give you solid, sensible advice on practical Western horsemanship that can help you and your horse for years to come.

101
WESTERN PLEASURE AND HORSEMANSHIP TIPS

Chapter 1

Horsemanship Fundamentals

Western riding may look easy, but that appearance is misleading. There's a subtle skill that goes along with its relaxed, comfortable style. It's good to gain some insight on horses and riding before ever putting your boot in the stirrup.

Horses can enjoy long careers and maintain their vitality if they are cared for properly.

Tip 1. Let your horse's health and soundness dictate his career.

Your horse is not a machine, so be attentive to the subtle changes he goes through during his life. As horses age, they may develop a few minor lameness issues that simply require a little maintenance (change of shoeing or diet, addition of supplements or medication) so that they can happily continue working at their current level. However, there are certain conditions (for example, laminitis or navicular or degenerative joint diseases) that may require you to adjust the intensity of his work, or even change what he does altogether. For example, a show horse that starts to develop DJD may not move well enough anymore for top competition, but he would be fine for local shows and pleasure riding.

Tip 2. Put your horse in a job he'll be successful in.

It's not fair to take a rocket scientist and make him into a dentist. The same goes with horses. If you want to compete in a particular class or event, or even if you're merely hoping to be successful in basic Western riding, make sure that your horse is capable of it. It doesn't take that rocket scientist to know that a horse bred and trained for Western pleasure probably won't be the ideal choice as a speed event horse. And if your dream is to have a steady-Eddie trail horse, maybe you shouldn't have bought a barrel racer. Resist forcing your horse into a job he doesn't have the aptitude for.

Tip 3. Groundwork is critical, but don't forget to ride.

There is one faction of Western riders that heartily believes "In Round Pen We Trust." After all, round-pen work is ideal to help develop a respectful relationship with your horse. Top trainers, legendary clinicians, and natural horsemanship gurus swear by them. And while round-penning and groundwork are important and helpful in establishing yourself as the herd leader, you still have to work on *your* riding ability. There are no substitutes for proper equitation and effective cueing from the saddle. All the "hooking-up" with your horse on the ground won't help you if you're unbalanced, have rough hands, swinging legs, and a weak position in the saddle.

Allow your horse some variety in his routine, such as tackling some obstacles on the trail course.

Tip 4. Keep variety in your program, whether you show or not.

While horses like routine, they don't want to be bored to death. So challenge your horse with a host of different activities. If you're strictly a recreational rider (you don't compete), you can still liven up your arena work with trail obstacles and ground poles. Get off the rail and practice patterns. Use cavaletti (elevated ground poles) to help your horse develop rhythm, improve his topline, and engage his hind end. And if you do have a show horse, you can improve his attitude by getting out of the arena altogether. Work on perfecting lead changes on the trail. Ride with a bunch of friends. Your horse will appreciate the different work from time to time.

You can have a wonderful friendship with your horse, as long as you are the wiser friend that he always turns to for advice.

Tip 5. Understanding relationship versus partnership.

Horsemen will say that it's important to have a partnership with the horse. This isn't entirely accurate. A partner by definition has an equal say in what is going on and can sometimes call the shots. A horse and rider should instead be better described as a solid working relationship. You, of course, are the empathic, sensitive, but decisive manager, while your horse is the eager, content, enthusiastic employee. You know how important it is to clearly communicate with your horse so that the business of riding is successful. You realize that it is important to coach your "employee" when necessary, to give encouragement and praise, and most importantly, when to get off his back. Your horse will reward you, as his leader, with a job well done.

Tip 6. When in doubt, check it out.

A horse that doesn't do what you're telling him to do probably has his reasons. It's up to you to do a little investigative work. Before you reach for a longer-shanked bit, a tie-down, draw reins, or other equipment, see if the problem has other origins. A horse may be "acting up" if he is uncomfortable or sore. Check out the three E's: Teeth, feet, and seat. If his teeth are bothering him, he will be stiff through the jaw and poll and may even carry his head awkwardly to alleviate the discomfort. A dental exam and regular floating can take care of this. His hooves can be another source of pain. Poor shoeing, stone bruises, and tender soles can all add up to a subtle lameness that makes a horse reluctant to cooperate. Finally, seat equals saddle. A poor-fitting saddle can cause a horse a world of hurt. If you suspect that your horse is suddenly not his happy self, have a professional horse person, whether that's a trainer or vet, take a closer look at him.

Tip 7. Ride a broke horse.

If you're just starting out, take the opportunity to ride a broke horse. No, it's not being suggested that you go out and buy a finished horse with perfect gaits. But wouldn't it be nice to sit on one for a day? Find a friend or trainer with a well-trained, nicely put together angel-on-hooves and spend an afternoon walking, jogging, loping, and cantering. Practice giving your cues and seeing the response. Gain a greater understanding of what it feels like to have all your aids understood. Remember that feeling. It will help if you try to re-create that on your own horse the next day.

One could spend a lifetime studying horses and still have much to learn. Here, equestrians get acquainted with a Quarter/Arab cross on the "Destination Equus" tour in Santa Ynez Valley, California.

Tip 8. Further your education.

It's great if you're taking some lessons from a capable trainer on a consistent basis. But your riding knowledge doesn't have to stop there. Going to horse expos, clinics, and seminars, watching DVDs, and reading books and magazines can not only help you keep abreast of current happenings in the Western horse world, they can also help you fine-tune your riding, or find solutions to current issues you might be having.

Chapter 2

Tack and Equipment

Your equipment makes a statement about you as a horse-man. The type of bridle and bit you select and the amount of training tack you use (or don't) speaks volumes for your skill with horses and knowledge of riding.

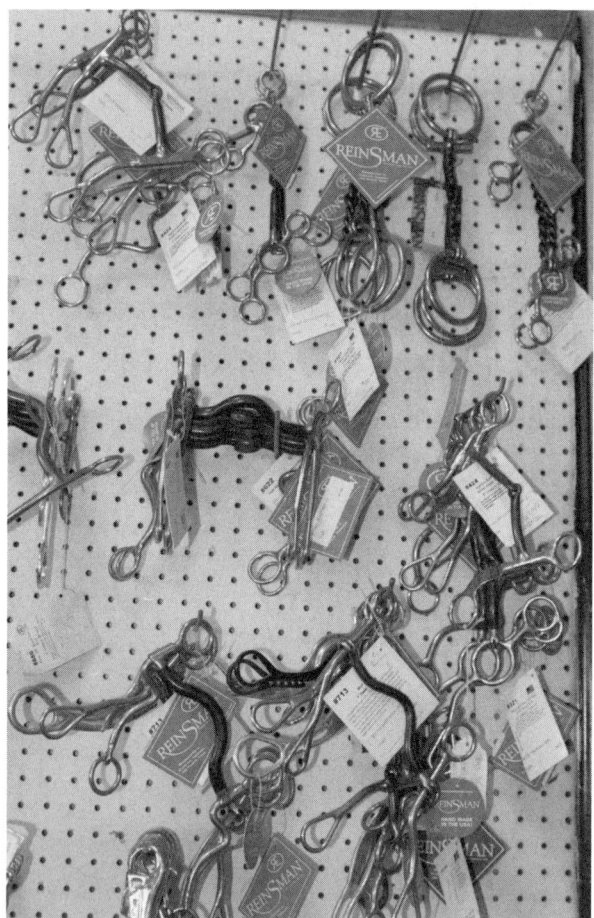

Even the most modest of tack stores will have a wide array of bits.
Stick to what your horse needs, not the latest fad.

Tip 9. Use as little equipment as you can to get the job done.

A visit to the tack shop is an intoxicating experience. All that gorgeous silver-appointed leather, the rows of ornate bits with various mouthpieces, the specialized saddles with matching accessories—delectable.

Does your horse need a tie-down? Should you get a breastplate that matches your saddle? What about that new curb bit with the fancy mouthpiece? Instead of just loading up your tack room with lots of unnecessary stuff, select items that help your horse work as comfortably and responsively as possible. For example, there are dozens of bits that could go between your horse's teeth—too many to mention here—but that doesn't mean that they are appropriate for him. O-ring snaffles or medium port curb bits are staples of the tack room. If your horse doesn't go well with one of them, have a horse professional help you figure out why. Don't just reach for the latest gadget.

A good working saddle will still keep its value over ultra trendy styles.

Tip 10. Pay for fit more than glitz.

When it comes to saddles, spend money on the part that matters the most to your horse: the saddle's fit. An ornate saddle dripping with silver doesn't do the horse any good if it causes him pain. When trying a saddle, avoid any contact with the horse's withers. When you sit in the saddle, slide your hand under the front edge of the saddle and feel for obvious finger pinching. The contact should be consistent all the way along the front—avoid gaps here and hard pressure there. For more advanced saddle fitting, consult an expert who can actually evaluate your horse's back and your intended purchase.

Spending money on fit rather than bling has its benefits. The best thing about a plain, well fitting saddle is that you can dress it up later as your budget allows. There are many different silver saddle trim sets to add on to your saddle. Everything from horn caps, cantle plates, corner plates, bars, and conchos are available whenever your checkbook has a few extra bucks in it.

Spurs are designed to allow the rider to refine the leg aids. Instead of constantly kicking, a touch with the spur will get the horse to listen. Spurs should never be used to punish the horse.

(A Roweled spur)

(Start with blunt, rounded tip spurs if you're just learning to use them)

Tip 11. Understand spurs.

Spurs can be useful for giving subtle cues to a horse and getting a quick response, but spurs are meant for the rider with a steady, practiced leg and a horse that understands leg pressure. If you decide to use spurs, start with rounded, gentle ones. Spurs with rowels come in various sizes and points and differ in severity. Remember that roweled spurs are meant to be used with a gentle roll, not a jab.

Saddle blankets come in all colors and a variety of materials from synthetic to wool.

Tip 12. Saddle blanket statements.

Your saddle blanket is the main contact between your saddle and the horse's back. When you remove your saddle blanket, always turn it inside out and allow it to air dry. Sunshine will kill bacteria that build up from sweat. Bang the blanket against the barn door or fence to knock dirt particles loose, and go over it with a synthetic brush to keep it from getting stiff. Make a point to hose down or dunk your wool blanket in water every month. Do your best to wring out the excess, then lay it over a fence rail. (Don't use soap: Soap can leave irritating residue in wool fibers.) Western saddles don't have any cushion built into them, so if you want to give your horse a little more protection, use a liner under your Navajo blanket. Liners can offer more shock absorbency than your blanket, they keep your blanket clean because the blanket doesn't contact a sweaty back, and they have a comfortable density to them.

Draw reins are an effective tool when used sparingly. They shouldn't be relied on, however, to train a proper headset.

Tip 13. Drawing the line on draw reins.

Draw reins might be a quick fix, or they might hide a simmering problem. A horse that is ridden constantly in draw reins begins to lean on them because he's not balanced, and the draw reins actually teach him that he can evade the bit. A better way is to ride him in a snaffle bit and use your natural aids: strong legs and sensitive hands. Focus on fine-tuning your transitions within the gaits, backing up, and circling to encourage him to round his back, lift his shoulders, and seek more bit contact.

Have patience when you are taking your horse's bridle off. Allow him to drop the bit on his own.

Tip 14. Unbridled care.

Allow your horse to accept or drop the bit of his own accord. Nothing makes a horse more reluctant to open wide for his bit than rough handling while bridling. Curb bits, particularly anything with a high port or spade mouthpiece, can not only be rough on the teeth, but can graze the palate when shoved into the mouth abruptly. When taking the bridle off, allow the horse to drop the bit on his own so that it isn't wrenched from his teeth.

Tip 15. **New saddle tips.**

A new saddle is a big investment. Because quality Western saddles are cut from thick, sturdy leather, they take some time to break in. To speed up the process, turn the stirrups one full turn in the direction that they will rest on your foot, then take a long broom handle and run it through the stirrup. This will help shape the fender so that you don't have to fish sideways for your stirrup while in the saddle. If the squeak of new leather is annoying to you when your horse moves, some horsemen suggest dusting the crevice between the skirts and the fenders with baby powder to dampen any too-new leather noises. However, some saddlemakers disagree with this old horseman's remedy and prefer that riders use a good leather conditioner *on the underside* of all the offending leather parts.

Tip 16. Inspect your gadget.

Draw reins and martingales can be useful for a short amount of time in certain scenarios and under certain conditions. But try not to rely on any artificial aid. You can really do damage to your training, not to mention your horse. People who constantly ride in draw reins artificially pull the horse's head down so much that the horse is constantly dragging along on his forehand. A running martingale distorts rein contact, so that when the rider picks up the reins, the martingale, which originates between the horse's front legs, applies downward pressure. Any time the rider takes off the martingale, the direct contact from rider's hand to bit is very different, and you'll need to reschool the horse to respond to your hand again.

Chapter 3.

Riding Basics

Western riding is most closely associated with the cattle ranches of the American West, but it also shares origins with the South American gaucho, the Mexican charro, the Spanish conquistador, and the Native American rider. Even with all these influences blending to a distinct riding style, every aspect of Western riding comes from the need to be efficient and secure while working in the saddle. If you learn the fundamentals of Western riding, you'll be gaining the wisdom of decades of horsemen before you.

A horse that has its fundamental building blocks of training is going to be light and responsive to your cues.

Tip 17. All horses need to have standard equipment.

Like a car, you'll get nowhere if your horse doesn't accelerate, brake, and steer. But unlike a car, you can't just push a pedal or adjust a wheel and expect results. Riders who kick to go and pull to stop are like a 3-year-old with keys to the Mercedes: They're not going very far. Make sure that you can get your horse to move immediately off your leg (using clear, correct cues) when asking him to go forward. In steering, remember that a good rider doesn't just pull the horse around by the head; instead the rider helps steer the entire body with legs and seat as well. Finally, a horse doesn't halt prettily, in balance, when he's yanked down to a stop. It's the combination of leg, seat, and then hand that fine-tunes the brakes. When you have control of speed, along with both sides of his body, getting where you want to go with your horse becomes much easier.

The correct position in the saddle should ultimately look natural and effortless.

Tip 18. Position is everything.

Correct posture in the saddle is not just for show riders. It allows you to control your horse effectively and give clear cues. If your position in the saddle is correct, then from the side view, you would be able to draw a straight line from the point of your shoulder, down through your hip, and finally to the back of your heel. Always think of sitting tall, with neither a curved spine nor an arch in your back. Keep your shoulders over your hips. Tall posture does not mean stiff, however. A rigid back can actually shorten the horse's stride.

To get your heels to stay down, don't just force them from the ankle. Sink your weight into your seat and think of pushing to the ground.

Tip 19. When in doubt, heels down.

How many times have you seen this scenario: A horse goes from a slow jog to a bone-jarring trot or even jumps into a canter, and the rider curls up on top of the horse like a boiled shrimp. The leg creeps up, the toe points down, and the body assumes a fetal position perched precariously atop the saddle. The reins become uselessly long.

Having a secure position in the saddle is key to successful riding, and a lot of that can start with getting your heels flexed down. If you find yourself in a spot where your horse is going a little too fast, sit up and sink your weight down into your stirrups. Think long leg. Sit on those seat pockets (your seat bones). You'll have much more control over your horse in this position. Certainly more than a shrimp.

A quick glance downward from time to time can tell you whether your leg is pushing into a chair position.

Tip 20. Save yourself from the chair.

One of the most common mistakes Western riders make is riding with their legs jutting too far in front of them—called the "chair seat." Riding with your legs in front of your center of gravity puts you slightly behind the motion of the horse. This seat constantly drives the horse. If you're trying to break the chair seat habit, make a point to look down over the front of your knee a couple times while you ride. You shouldn't be able to see more than the tip of your boot—any more and your leg is too far forward.

Turning your toe slightly out will help the muscles along your entire leg make contact.

Tip 21. Tune up your leg position.

A good leg position isn't just about equitation. It's your anchor in the saddle, as well as your communication station. Keep balanced in the saddle by distributing your weight evenly between your seat and the balls of your feet in the stirrups. Turn your feet out at a very slight angle, rather than pointed straight forward. A foot in the forward position takes the calf away from the horse, making communication less effective. Turning the foot out slightly closes the upper thigh and lower leg against the horse's side.

Left) two-handed split reins; Center) romal reins; and Right) one-handed split reins for curb bridle.

Tip 22. Hold your reins properly.

Depending on the kind of bridle you use, you have a couple of different options for the way you'll hold your reins. If you're using split reins and riding two-handed, you can cross them or bridge them, as follows: Cross the right rein over the left side of your horse's neck and the left rein over the right side, then pick up the doubled reins, one in each hand, with your thumbs resting on top of the reins, thumbnails facing up.

When riding one-handed in a curb bridle with split reins, hold both reins in your left hand, with your index finger between the two pieces of leather. Your fingers will curl down, while your knuckles face the sky. For romal reins, have the reins come through your left hand from the bottom. Then hold the romal (the joined ends that go into one long quirt) in the right hand against your thigh.

Top: The right way to neck rein: the left hand is held up and moves over slightly—you can tell that the left rein is against the neck by the shadow cast by the right rein as it moves away from the neck. Bottom: Pulling the hand down and over is a common mistake.

Tip 23. Neck reining without pressure.

A challenge for riders just starting out is coordinating their neck reining cues without making overly dramatic gestures that the horse will feel in the mouth. When neck reining your horse one-handed, think of moving your rein hand slightly toward your horse's right ear for a left turn and his left ear for a right turn. This slight movement lays the opposite rein on the horse's neck, telling him which direction you would like to go, without applying any pressure to the bit.

By having a light touch on the reins, you can use the sensitive fingertips to communicate with your horse.

Tip 24. Finesse your feel on the reins.

When you ride two-handed, use your fingers as well as your palms to establish a good feel on the reins. This allows you to use subtle movement to tell your horse exactly what you want in slight cues. Instead of using the entire weight and strength of your arm to cue or control your horse, which ends up being harsh on his mouth, try to isolate your cue to just your wrist. Use wrist motion alone to apply rein pressure, rather than moving your arm, elbows, and shoulders.

Close your eyes for a few strides and feel your position. This rider shows balance and a beautiful position.

Tip 25. Closed-eye balancing act.

To check that you're balanced left to right in the saddle, ask your horse for a quiet walk or jog along the arena rail. When your horse is settled and moving along without a fuss, close your eyes for several yards. Feel your seat bones. Do you have equal weight in the left seat bone versus the right? Now feel your feet in the stirrups. Are you putting more pressure in one than the other? Because humans naturally have a dominant side, it's important to check that you're riding evenly on a regular basis, and closing your eyes allows you to zero in on "feel."

Riders with longer legs have to resist lifting up the heel to kick. Here the rider has turned the toe out to nudge the horse with his entire leg.

Tip 26. Leg contact gets your point across.

Cueing the Western horse to move forward isn't a big yee-haw experience. Some riders get into the poor habit of kicking their horse in a way that lifts the entire leg away from the horse. To cue your horse or give him a nudge without throwing off your balance, turn your toe out more than usual, which will bring your calf against his side. You can then push or nudge him while keeping your knee and thigh in contact with the saddle.

Here the rider turns her head right, but still keeps her body position forward. Her horse follows the bend of the circle, without falling in.

Tip 27. Isolate your body parts in the saddle.

Your ability to cue your horse depends on how well you can give your aids. You have to be able to use your various body parts independently. So try to isolate your movements, such as lifting your hand without moving your shoulder. Move your lower calf back behind the cinch without swinging your entire leg. Turn your head without twisting your upper body.

A relaxed hand and elbow gives the rider more sensitivity on the reins.

Tip 28. Have a hand at relaxation.

Keep your elbows bent and wrists straight and relaxed. There should be an invisible line from your elbow to the horse's mouth. If your arms are stiff, you won't be able to do any subtle cueing or offer any of the give and take that's necessary to effectively "converse" with your horse.

There's no need to hold the reins any tighter than just keeping enough feel so that they don't slip from your hand.

Tip 29. Eliminate the fists of fury.

Keep your hand closed on your reins, but don't hold them in a tight fist. It causes stiffness through the arm and shoulder, which makes your hand insensitive and may cause your horse to become tense or stiff through the jaw. Keep slightly open fingers on the rein and a light touch—but don't hold them so loosely that the reins slip out of your hand or constantly need adjusting. You need to have good feel on the reins, but not a white-knuckled grip.

Check to see that you aren't leaning to one side or riding with one stirrup longer than the other.

Tip 30. Shoulder the work.

Try to keep your shoulders level and aligned. A slumped position or a dropped shoulder may result in uneven weight distribution. If you feel yourself consistently tipping or leaning to one side, check to see if your stirrups are even. Your horse may also travel crookedly, which is causing you to lean with him. If you are riding with too much weight on one side, drop that stirrup and ride with the other one only. Stretch up and elongate your torso, and keep those shoulders naturally back.

Tip 31. Strong legs equal good balance.

Build up your riding muscles and resist having to rely on your stirrups for balance. Practice dropping and picking up your stirrups without looking—it's tough at first. Then ride without stirrups, but keep the correct leg position, right down to your lowered heels. You'll have to depend on your muscles to keep you in the proper position. Finally, try standing in your stirrups while your horse is trotting. Try not to pinch at the knee, but instead use the whole of your leg from lower calf to upper thigh. The more you practice, the more your balance increases and your reliance on the saddle horn decreases.

Chapter 4

Success at any Speed: Your Horse's Gaits

Your horse should always move with an easy, smooth rhythm. The gaits may seem slow, but the objective is to have a horse that is a pleasure to ride effortlessly. Learn how to perfect your horse's walk, jog, and lope, and even work on some lateral moves. Success is all about harmony, balance, and a good working relationship.

Use a light touch on the rein when suppling your horse at the halt. He'll soon understand what you want.

THE WALK

Tip 32. Use your first minutes in the saddle to supple your horse.

A horse that is flexible laterally will also be able to respond better to your aids and accept the bit. At the halt, hold one rein in each hand, then smoothly pick up contact on the right rein and direct the horse's head and neck to the right. Do this in a quiet manner; don't just yank the horse's head over. If your horse begins to walk in a circle, you've pulled too hard or too quickly. Settle your horse back at a halt, then try again. Once your horse has turned his head to the furthest point he is comfortable giving you, release the rein as smoothly as you picked it up. Allow your horse to carry his head and neck back to "center." Then relax that rein while picking up contact on the left rein to direct his head smoothly to the left. Continue to supple the horse with your reins. Most horses will be flexible enough after just a few sessions to nearly touch a nose to your toe.

Suppling your horse with your inside rein while you circle gets your
horse loosened up and isolates his body parts.

Tip 33. Circle to help activate the hindquarters.

Further help your horse improve his walk by incorporating small circles into your warm-up. Ride two-handed and cue your horse to walk forward on a straight line. Then apply steady pressure on your right rein to steer your horse right and onto a small circle. Keep the horse moving actively by applying your inside leg at the cinch, and prevent your horse's hindquarters from drifting out by keeping your outside leg (left) well behind the cinch. After a couple circles, allow your horse to walk forward, and then reverse your aids and circle the other direction.

Don't forget to use your legs to keep your horse walking forward.

Tip 34. Learn to keep your cues going.

Even though you're using your reins to tell your horse what you want, you still need to remember to use your other aids. Don't let your horse's energy level drop just because you pick up contact with your reins. Keep your horse going actively with your leg and seat and drive him up to the bridle.

Keeping the lower back soft transfers through your entire body.

Tip 35. Don't be a working stiff.

While your horse is walking, keep your lower back soft. Move with the horse's motion by allowing your pelvis to work like a hinge, connecting your quiet legs to your upper body. If you tense your lower back and become stiff, it transfers to your horse as tension, and the walk will shorten and slow.

Tip 36. Do the bump (with your heel).

If your horse is shuffling along at the walk, try to increase his energy by bumping him, with each heel alternating. Horses often become dull to constant squeezing pressure, and a hard kick will most likely cue him into a jog. Keep the rhythm that you'd like your horse to be moving in, and make your heel bumps definite and rhythmical. Eventually your horse will pick up your rhythm and improve his speed. When he does, reward him by immediately stopping the bumping action.

Tip 37. Keep your horse on the straight and narrow.

As you're walking, you want your horse to be traveling in a straight line, not zigzagging like a drunken bar patron. Take a rein in each hand and hold both reins low to teach him correct body alignment. Think of working on a large square, instead of a circle (you can use four markers as cones). At the walk, head toward your first cone. The moment you feel your horse start drifting off your path, pick up your aids to set him back on track. For example, if he drifts left, block him with your left leg, lay the left rein against his neck, use an opening rein low on his right side, and guide him back into a straight line. When he returns to his path, redistribute your leg and hand pressure evenly. When you come up to your square's corner, look at your new path, use your outside leg and rein to support the turn, and then go back to even aids. Your horse will get used to following an intended path when you can help him focus and plan ahead.

Back the horse so that he transfers his weight to his hindquarters and rounds over his back.

Tip 38. Know whoa.

If your horse doesn't stop promptly when you ask by applying light and even pressure on the reins, putting weight in your seat, and giving a crisp verbal "whoa," improve his stop by asking him to rapidly back up for several steps after every mediocre stop. Soon he'll be shifting his weight to his hind end and stopping promptly whenever you ask.

A horse doesn't just bend at the neck. He can carry the bend through his entire body.

Tip 39. Arc de triumph.

When you turn your horse in a circle, it shouldn't just be only his head and neck that bend while his body stays stiff; his entire body should arc, matching the shape of the circle. If your horse has trouble with this, remember that your legs must guide his body into the correct shape—leg at the cinch to move his shoulders, leg slightly behind the cinch to move his hind end. Whichever end is out of place, your legs can help align it.

Use gentle alternating pressure to keep the bit moving in the horse's mouth so that he soon yields to the bit.

Tip 40. Achieve a soft jaw without a hard bump.

A horse may set his jaw against the bit, making him resistant to your cues. Get rid of resistance without having to bump him drastically in the mouth. Don't just pull back in hard, long tugs. A horse will always win this sort of tug of war. Your goal is to soften him up to the bit. Riding two-handed, "massage" the bit in his mouth by moving it gently and smoothly with the reins. He can't set his jaw to the bit when it is moving constantly in this slight, subtle motion. When you feel him relax and yield to the bit, ease up on your rein aids. Go back to the gentle massage when you feel him brace again. Soon he'll learn to give freely to your hand.

Your horse should travel close to the rail, but not push your leg into it.

Tip 41. Just scraping by.

If your horse tends to run your leg into the rail or other objects, avoid the common mistake of pulling his head away from the rail or object. If you do that, you're actually allowing his shoulder and body to move closer to the object. Instead, turn his head toward the object, which will bend him slightly, moving his shoulder and body away and saving your leg.

Tip 42. Go bare if you dare.

Riding bareback not only helps develop an independent seat and great balance, it also allows you to understand the horse's gaits and movement better. Use a bareback pad for you and your horse's comfort (unless the horse truly is mutton withered or built like an armchair), and ride only in the arena at first to get used to the newfound freedom. Keep it to a walk, then ask for a little jog with a slight squeeze. Anytime you feel insecure, go back down to the walk. Once you feel balanced and confident, ask for the lope. It is a liberating feeling to ride saddleless!

THE JOG

Tip 43. A long stride can be a blessing.

A horse with a longer stride shouldn't be penalized for his jog, because it can translate into a comfortable, free-flowing gait. You can still have him collect, yet carry himself, without constantly pulling him by his mouth into an artificial slowness. If your horse has a long-strided jog, ride two-handed and keep a friendly feel on both reins—you're not pulling your horse in, but your reins aren't flopping idly either. Put even leg pressure against the horse's sides and try to push him into the contact. Then start making 90-degree turns to the right or left, or good-sized circles. Circles will force your horse to rebalance himself and shift his weight to his hind end.

Try to feel the two different motions that the horse is creating as he jogs.

Tip 44. Control the bouncy jog.

To help sit an active jog better, think of the gait's characteristics. It has an up and down motion, sure, but try to feel how both diagonal pairs of legs are moving in unison as well. Because the jog has side-to-side movement as well as the bouncy up and down, you can absorb the movement of the horse by moving left/right, left/right as well as up/down (however, be careful not to overly exaggerate these movements).

Put your horse into a jog and at first don't do anything—just bounce along for a couple strides. Then try to feel the lateral motion of the gait. As you begin to move your seat bones with the motion, sitting a bouncy jog can actually be done effectively and effortlessly.

A horse with a bouncy jog can often make it tough for a rider to sit for extended lengths of time.

Tip 45. Reduce your air time.

After several minutes at the jog, riders often tire and start to bounce up out of the saddle. Allow your seat to find the saddle by tightening your abdominals inward, as if you're trying to push your belly button into your spine. This will help drive your seat bones south so that they can rest comfortably in the saddle. Also, drop your stirrups and practice sitting in a deep, shock-absorbing seat. Not relying on stirrups forces you to feel the jog and relax into it.

Extend the jog into a long trot, letting the horse step well underneath himself and flow in his gait, and then you'll be able to collect him back down to a more active jog.

Tip 46. The long trot helps the jog.

If your horse has a really choppy jog (and even a disjointed lope), you can improve it by first allowing him to extend into a long trot. Move your horse into the jog and then ask for more impulsion by giving strong squeezes or even a roll of your spur. Do not restrict him with the bridle. Try to get him to engage his hind end and really push and reach with his hind legs. It will not only help freshen up his gaits, but will also improve his collected jog because he is not artificially shuffling—he's actually learned to use his body. Then continue to ask with your legs, but take a little feel of both reins. Release the rein pressure, then add it again. This type of contact will help him regulate his speed down to the jog, with the same rhythm and cadence he had at the extended trot.

Jogging can be tough if a horse is just learning to do it correctly. Let him take walk breaks, but make sure it's an active walk.

Tip 47. Take a break.

If you are doing a lot of collected jog work, be sure to give your horse a break. Collected work is strenuous, particularly if your horse is just learning how to use his hind end and work his topline muscles. Take a few trips around the arena and then transition down to an extended walk, really pushing him to reach into the bridle. He'll appreciate the opportunity to stretch out, and you are still asking him to create energy from behind. Then pick up your reins and collect him back to the jog. Brightening his gait will enhance his overall cadence and rhythm.

Tip 48. Bridle reins don't make your horse go.

You see it plenty in Western movies—riders who urge their horses on by spanking them across the shoulders with the long ends of their split reins. Looks good and adds to the excitement, doesn't it? However, it's not an effective way to tell the horse to move forward. One of the main reasons is because when riders flip the reins around, they often jab the horse in the mouth with their flailing hands, giving the horse mixed signals. Another reason to not use the reins is because the shoulder is not the right place to ask for speed—that's not his engine. Reins are meant to help communicate with the horse. They are not an artificial aid. If you do need to get your horse to move promptly forward and your leg isn't cutting it, carry a crop or a bat, and apply it behind your leg, near his hind end.

Tip 49. **Keep moving along.**

Your horse seems to run out of gas the minute he starts loping. If you've ruled out that there is no physical reason for your horse to be breaking out of his lope and you've cued him correctly, you need to let him know that when to quit is not his decision to make. It goes back to his responsiveness: He must move smartly off your aids and keep going until you tell him to stop. (A good rider, however, is sensitive to the horse's stamina—he can't keep loping if he's out of shape.)

Squeeze him back into a lope, and the moment he breaks, give him a sharp tap behind your leg with a crop. Praise him even if he overreacts and leaps forward—you can always slow him down after a few strides.

Keep that crop handy, and remember to always apply it behind your leg, where his energy comes from.

Cue for the lope correctly and you'll have the horse lift his shoulder, (push from his hind end and reach for the contact.)

Tip 50. How to ask for the lope.

You've selected the perfect place to ask for a lope, except that when you ask, you get a bone-jarring, filling-loosening trot. To correctly ask for the lope, you need to use hand, leg, and seat. First, take a slight feel of your reins, and then move him up into the bridle with even pressure from both legs. Don't let him step off yet, though. You're creating energy so he can push off from his hindquarters. Then take a tiny bit more contact on your inside rein, put weight in your seat bones, keep your inside leg at the girth, and give a distinct and definite squeeze with your lower outside leg. Your horse should step right into the lope—if instead he trots, just bring him right down to the walk again and ask again, with a little more conviction with that outside leg. Once he does lope, get off his face and allow him to lope freely for several strides. Then allow him to walk, give him a pat, and ask for the lope again. Do this a few times in a row so that he understands not just the cues for the lope, but *your* way of asking him.

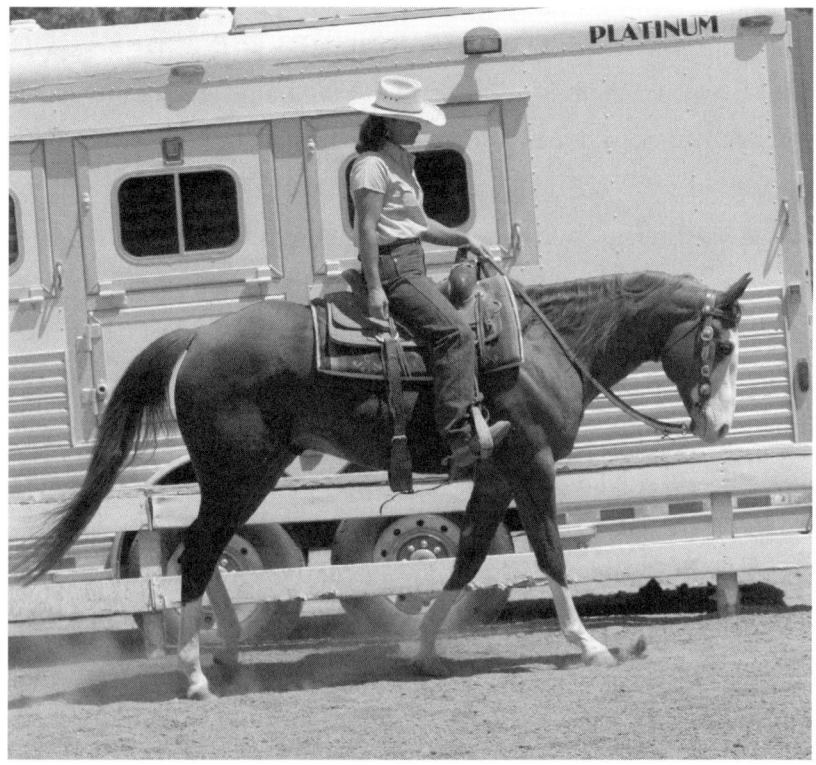

When you check to see what lead you are on, a mere glance downward is enough. If you tilt your body forward, you will throw yourself and your horse slightly off balance.

Tip 51. Take the lead on feeling leads.

It's important that you know your leads through feel before you start to show. If your horse does take a wrong lead during a class, you must quickly correct it. There's nothing that shouts beginner louder than someone who lets his horse lope round and round the show pen on the wrong lead! As your horse lopes, look down to see which shoulder is leading, then file that "feel" away in your head. Quiz yourself whenever you pick up your lope, by guessing whether he is on the right lead or not, then look down to "check your answer."

Tip 52. Keep your horse between your leg and reins.

If you feel your horse is running through your hand at the lope, try this exercise. As he lopes, sink your weight into your seat, close your legs, and apply light pressure to both reins. You want to feel the horse compress his frame slightly, lift up his front end, and round his back ever so slightly. Then continue to push him into the bit with hand and supporting leg until he halts. Once he's stopped, move the bit back and forth in his mouth and squeeze him with your legs until he backs up. Keep the bit fluid in his mouth—he won't be able to build up resistance. When he does what you asked, release your aids almost completely, but still keep a little rein contact. Take up the contact again, and ask him to back up. You should feel him continue to lift his shoulders and sink over his hocks. Have him stop, pat him, and then lope off. This will help tune up his responsiveness to your aids.

Tip 53. **The buck stops here.**

When you ask for the lope, if your horse decides that he would rather give you a little buck, bolt off, or kick out at your leg, you may be giving him mixed signals. Examine how you are giving him cues with your leg. You might be asking him too abruptly, bumping him hard with your spur, using more leg than necessary, or bringing your leg in too quickly.

Ask for the lope on a circle, and keep him on a large circle for a few rounds until he understands that you want him to stay on that lead.

Tip 54. Circling in on the correct lead.

If your horse has trouble picking up his leads (and health issues have been ruled out), practice asking him to lope on a circle until he learns his cues. In a circle, he will naturally want to pick up the inside leg to stay balanced.

Tip 55. Speed control.

You can rate your horse's lope if you can get him to pay attention to your position in the saddle and the way you shift your weight. When you are loping fast and would like to slow down, you should bring your rein hand back toward your body and sit deeper in the saddle. Sit upright instead of leaning forward and relax; think about deepening your seat and almost melting into the saddle. To assist your horse in understanding your cue, choose an area to make a circle in, and then look where you want to go and guide your horse onto that circle. If you stay relaxed and tall, while sitting deeply with light rein contact, your horse will slow. Anytime he gets a little fast, put him on a circle smoothly and quietly—don't yank or cue abruptly.

Tip 56. Remember how much bit you have.

If your horse gets rambunctious at the lope and takes off running, it's hard not to want to haul on his face to stop him. In your hurry to get him back under control, keep in mind what kind of hardware you have between his teeth. A high port curb is very severe when roughly used, and some horses have literally been pulled off their feet in re-action to a harsh yank on the reins. If your loping horse becomes too fast, use a smooth give and take on the reins to rate his speed. Not enough? You're on a freight train? Take one of your reins and pull that runaway into a circle. Again, if he's carrying a really strong bit, use just enough pressure to get the job done. Don't cause him to lose his balance and fall.

Straightness is a hallmark of a sound, well-trained horse who knows how to use his body correctly.

Tip 57. Be straightforward when you lope.

Your horse may be hugging the rail, but he's traveling at an angle. A horse that lopes off crookedly, or lopes with haunches canted in, doesn't have enough inside leg support to keep him straight on the rail. Riding two-handed, ask your horse for the lope. If he does one of his customary drifts, immediately use your inside lower leg at the cinch to get back on track. Think of your inside leg as a wall that he can't blast through.

Tip 58. Drifting in at the lope.

Sometimes horses take advantage of their riders and start to cut corners and drift into the center of the ring at the lope. You have to correct him immediately. If he's on his left lead and he begins to lean in before he actually turns, get after him then. Riding two-handed, use a strong outside rein to direct him back over to the rail, supporting him with your inside leg, then let him go. The second he drifts again, repeat the correction. He'll soon learn that he's not going to decide when he can go to the center of the arena.

Tip 59. Onward, not upward.

When you cue your horse to lope from the walk and instead he tosses his head, backs up, or even rears, you might be restricting him with your hand too much, leaving him nowhere to go (but up, in many cases). While your first instinct might be to tighten your grip on your reins when you are also asking him to go, he still needs that door opened if he is to get his engine in gear. Ask with your leg, soften your hand, and allow him to freely push forward from behind. After he is loping, you can then make slight adjustments in your rein and seat cues to perfect his speed.

It's ok if your horse backs up crookedly if he's locked up and going nowhere. The point is to just get him moving first, then you can finesse it.

BACKING UP

Tip 60. The key to unlocking your backup.

If your horse tends to lock up and freeze when you ask him to back, try unlocking him by applying give and take pressure to one rein more than the other. This bending may mean he backs crookedly, but it will unlock him and get him moving. At first just ask for a step or two, release your rein, and give him praise. Once your horse understands that you'd like some movement backwards, you can tweak your backing cues and return to asking him to back straight.

Here a horse is backing up beautifully. There's no fight, and there's no dragging by the mouth. Horses rarely back up in nature.

Tip 61. Two steps forward, one step back.

If your horse will not back up under saddle, you will have to make his feet move somewhere. An alternative to going backward is side to side. Don't just keep pulling on his face, but instead focus on moving his feet and letting him relax into the bridle—he'll round his back and lift his shoulder as he moves side to side. Then ask him to go forward while picking up the rein contact; apply slight rein pressure but make him take a step backward with leg pressure and a deep seat. If he takes even one step without evading the bit, release your aids and pat him. Then ask again. He'll soon back with very little fuss.

Tip 62. A good backup plan.

Most people mistakenly teach their horse to back up by picking up on the reins and applying pressure to the horse's face until they're dragging the horse backwards, his mouth gaping and feet shuffling. You can teach the horse to back up better under saddle by first teaching the horse to back from the ground. Using a halter, lead rope, and a dressage whip, stand at his shoulder facing backward, apply pressure to the nose, and tap the chest of the horse very lightly. When he takes a step back, reward him by releasing the pressure and taps. Repeat your aids, always releasing them when he does what you say. Gradually increase the number of steps he takes back.

ADVANCED MOVEMENTS

Tip 63. Turn it over.

For sideways movements or turns, keep in mind that leg pressure at the cinch will be most effective for moving your horse's shoulder, while pressure applied slightly behind the cinch will move his hips and hind end.

Use the fence in front of you to help your horse sidepass. Make sure you don't let those hindquarters trail behind—they should be leading the way as seen in this rear view.

Tip 64. The sidepass.

Use your arena fence and have your horse stand right in front of it so that the fence blocks any forward movement (rather than you having to use strong rein pressure). Take an even feel of both reins and push with your outside leg. If you are going to the right, take your right leg completely away from the horse's side and then start with a light pressure of your left leg try to push him over. Add more leg if he ignores you. Bump him with your heel until he takes a step sideways. When he does it correctly for a couple steps, stop, pat, and then ask again. Change your aids so that the horse sidepasses to the left as well.

If the horse is crossing well with his legs, but leading with his shoulder, use your outside leg to move his haunches over.

Tip 65. A straight pass.

If your horse can't stay straight during the sidepass, you'll have to help him along. He should never lead with his shoulder; instead, his first steps should come from his hips. If you find your horse bulging, say to the right with his right shoulder, pick up contact with your outside (left) rein to straighten out his neck, head, and shoulder, then offer better support with your leg, well behind the cinch.

The key to a turn on the haunches is that the horse keeps moving around his back pivot foot.

Tip 66. **One good turn.**

In order to execute a turn on the haunches, first start out at the walk and put your horse on a small circle. As you complete the circle, make the next one smaller, and then the next one even smaller, using your outside leg firmly to push him into an arc. The horse will have to shift his weight to his hindquarters, and once he does give him the cue to halt, but keep pushing firmly with your outside leg until he begins to pivot. Praise him, let him relax and walk forward, then repeat the exercise. Only when your horse has full understanding of what you're asking and he's giving you pretty much a 180-degree turn on the haunches should you reverse and try it in the other direction.

Chapter 5.

Western Pleasure Essentials

If you want to do more than merely "ride Western," the pleasure class division is probably what you're looking for. Western pleasure is the most popular rail class in all of the Western divisions; it's not complicated to get started in, and there are classes at all levels, from schooling shows all the way up to World shows. But it does have a distinct set of rules you must be true to if you want to have success.

A good Western pleasure horse is a tremendous equine athlete.

Tip 67. The athletic pleasure horse.

You may think that a Western pleasure horse doesn't have a demanding job, moving slowly around the ring. But walking, jogging, and loping slowly in a correct frame—the hind legs reaching under the horse—takes a great deal of physical development. Always strive to have your horse move correctly, stepping underneath himself. This may mean work at the extended trot or going faster during the walk, jog, and lope than you would ultimately like; however, your horse must work toward traveling correctly while traveling slowly. At first he may only be able to maintain correct movement in a correct frame at slower speeds for a short period of time before you have to move him out so that he continues to step underneath himself. Be patient, and remember he must build his physical fitness.

A good rider will keep their eyes up and looking ahead, watching all that is around them with their peripheral vision.

Tip 68. Fix your gaze.

One mistake many riders make is looking down at their horse's head-set. Winning riders look where they're going, not down at their horse's head. Get used to having soft eyes that can take in your horse and surroundings without requiring you to dip your head and look down. Remember that horses will go in the direction you're looking, because subtle body changes will indicate to him where your attention is.

It's a shame that the lope has suffered from such a bad reputation in years previous. A quality lope shows lightness and balance, being a true pleasure to ride.

Tip 69. Let your horse lope.

The lope is one of the most misconstrued gaits for a Western pleasure horse. In an effort to keep horses slow, you'll see plenty of horses canted along the rail, haunches in, as their riders try to artificially force slowness. There will be some horses that are four-beating: loping in front and jogging behind. Don't be one of those riders who shuts his horse down. Quality of gait is essential to the true pleasure horse. Do your homework before getting to the show so that your horse is driving well from behind and truly loping.

Today's Western pleasure horse doesn't carry the peanut-roller head of the past, but instead has the distinct level topline and headset that will become the standard for years to come.

Tip 70. From the judge's chair.

If you're working toward showing in Western pleasure classes, it makes sense to understand what judges look for. A top-notch pleasure horse is a good mover with three distinct gaits. He walks in a steady rhythm with smooth, even footfalls. His jog comes from lifting through his front shoulder and stepping well under himself with his hind legs. There is very little knee and hock action, but rather a relaxed, collected pace that is not artificially forced to be slow. The lope has three distinct beats, where the horse's legs sweep the ground. The horse doesn't raise his knees up, but is balanced and moving from the hip. A good loper pushes well from behind to carry himself with impulsion.

The Western pleasure horse's signature is its level topline. The horse's frame should be like the horizon: poll, neck, wither, and croup all level. In years past, horses were trained to carry their heads unnaturally low, but that has changed in recent years.

Obviously, there are horses blessed with the ideal conformation and movement, and they will have an advantage over competitors that don't. However, if the rider knows how to present the horse at his finest, that pair will have an excellent chance of bringing home the blue.

The ideal headset still gives the rider and horse some flexibility to be natural for its conformation.

Tip 71. The ideal topline and headset.

The Western pleasure horse will have a totally level topline from his poll to his croup, and will carry his nose a few inches naturally in front of the vertical. He shouldn't have his nose jutting out further than about 5 inches though, because it will appear as though he's trying to evade the bit. You also don't want a horse that is low and behind the vertical, looking intimidated. A horse that carries himself in a frame with a relaxed, natural head position will really wow the judge.

Tip 72. More judging insight.

Your horse is not merely judged on his three gaits—he could be a good mover but still not place in the ribbons. This is because the horse is also judged on his transitions to and from those gaits. A horse that goes willingly into the next gait will impress the judge. The horse should not anticipate the next gait or be resistant to your cues when you do ask him to jog or lope. The horse should also be able to lope without taking trot steps beforehand.

Tip 73. Western pleasure myths.

A lot of people think that the bit gives the Western pleasure horse his headset. They think that using a high port curb will make the horse carry his head a certain way. But to easily dispel this myth, notice the snaffle bit babies and horses shown in bosals. A good headset is part conformation and part training, but has very little to do with the type of bit in the horse's mouth.

It's fine to make adjustments to bridle your horse up, but constantly nagging your horse about his headset doesn't do any good if you don't ride the rest of the horse, too.

Tip 74. The whole horse needs to be in a frame.

Too many people obsess with their horse's head position and forget about the rest of the horse! They are constantly fussing and pulling with their hands, and by the time they have the head where they want it, they've lost the horse's engine. They restrict the horse from going anywhere. A good Western pleasure horse is always moving forward in a true frame.

Tip 75. **Temporary headset help.**

If you are looking to fine-tune your horse's headset for the show pen, keep your artificial training aids to a minimum—a little goes a long way. But some trainers suggest a sidepull (a lightweight, bitless headstall that works through direct pressure on the nose) and a training fork (a modified running martingale) to temporarily help the horse understand what you're after. Attach the training fork to your cinch, run it between the horse's front legs, and run the bridle reins through its rings. You want it to be adjusted very loosely—you *never* want to actually pull your horse's head down. You are not training the horse to drop his head, but rather defining the boundaries of where his head shouldn't go.

Tip 76. No ducking out.

If your horse is ducking behind the bit, he's going to be able to evade your aids. A horse that is traveling with his chin tucked in is not relaxed in the bridle and accepting your cues. Use this exercise: Switch out to a milder bit—like a snaffle if you normally ride in a curb—and remove your reins. Put his saddle on him, then take him to the round pen. Allow him to move freely around the edge of the pen, then ask him for a big trot, letting him stretch out as he pleases with no association of pressure on the reinless bit. Then attach your reins, mount up, and under saddle, move him from his collected lope into a big canter, but stay off his face completely. Once he can extend his gaits in the security of the round pen, his nose and frame will stretch forward.

Tip 77. The spur stop.

Some pleasure horses are schooled in the spur stop, where the rider, not wanting to take up any rein contact in front of the judge to rate the horse's gaits, will teach the horse to respond to the use of the spur in order to regulate—or even stop—him. The judge expects you to feel your horse's mouth and have communication. The spur stop has turned into just another trick for getting a response. True riding comes from a classic position: heels down, legs on, and spurs out of the horse's sides. While the spur stop is effective in the show pen, it is a gimmick, and many horsemen frown upon it.

Chapter 6.

Getting Ready to Show

Being competitive about your riding can be very fulfilling. You're not only testing yourself against the ideals of the division, you're also pitting yourself against your peers. It's good to have some general background about competing in horse shows before sending in your first entry form.

Your local tack store will often have a bulletin board posting local shows. If you're just starting out, it's a good place to seek out schooling shows.

Tip 78. Select the type of show that is right for your level.

Don't be paying all the expensive fees for a big-time regional show if you're just starting out. Instead, cut your teeth at a schooling show. You can get all the benefits of competing against your peers with the potential added bonus (depending upon the judge) of feedback. Some judges will actually give you tips and advice in the show pen at lineup, while others will allow you to approach them during breaks.

And if you're well beyond that level, challenge yourself. If your horse is registered, you can conquer the breed show circuit. You can also hit up many of the state and regional championships, and even start qualifying for National and World shows. Do what you can to make your show experience enjoyable, yet challenging, for you and your horse.

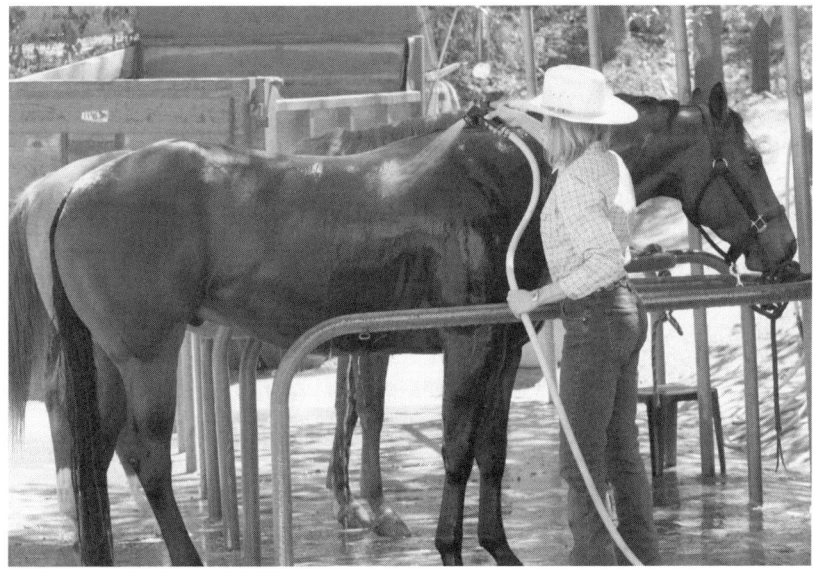

Your pre-show bath should take place the day before.

Tip 79. Grooming your horse for the show pen.

Horses should be immaculate when presented in their classes. Clip bridle path, ears (inside and out), muzzle, and long feeler hairs around the eyes. Trim up coronets (be careful on white legs, however, so you don't create blade marks). Pull the mane so that it is thin and about four inches in length.

The day before your show, bathe your horse using an equine shampoo (specially formulated for their pH). For an added boost, select a shampoo that enhances color—gray horses benefit the most from a whitening shampoo. Follow with mane and tail conditioner, and use an ample amount. Scrub any chrome (white areas) down to the pink skin beneath.

Let your horse dry, and add a coat sheen product everywhere but the saddle area. A detangler will make your horse's tail flow beautifully. Show horses generally have their long tails blunt-cut at the bottom. Add some hair mousse to the mane to make it easy to handle, and band the horse's mane. Using extra small bands to match your horse's color, place a band around a half-inch section of mane, at the base right by the roots. The result is a beautifully groomed horse, with his conformation accentuated, that looks finished.

Tip 80. Take a test drive.

If you have never taken your horse to a show, one of the best ways to see how your horse will behave is to haul him to an event without entering. The commotion of the show grounds will be the same whether you have paid your entry fees or not, and it gives you a chance to get your horse used to the atmosphere. Tack up and get on and just take a leisurely walk around the warm-up areas and arenas. Have your horse stand near the in-gate if possible to get accustomed to the noise of the announcer's booth, the sight of the judge's box, and the activity of show horses moving everywhere.

Tip 81. Remember the little tasks.

The night before the show, take care of the details. Clean your saddle and bridle. Make sure your silver is polished to perfection. Your boots should be cleaned and your show outfit put together. You'll show the judge that you are serious about your show career, and you and your horse will contribute a beautiful overall picture to the sport.

Having a friend at the show is not only helpful, it's great moral support.

Tip 82. Support groups can be a lifesaver.

It's hard managing everything at a show by yourself. That's why it's such a benefit to have—at the very least—one friend who can help you pick up your number at the show office, groom your horse for a class, tack up, give your boots a good dusting off before you go in the ring, and hold your horse during your bathroom breaks. Besides being helpful, a good friend will be your most ardent cheering section too.

Small details make a big impression, including using hoof polish. Today's hoof black products are not harsh and can be left to wear off naturally.

Tip 83. It's (almost) show time.

Before going into your class, add these final touches. Make dark hooves shiny with lacquer and hoof black (use clear, if feet are light). Use a spray sheen product over the horse's body. You can accentuate the horse's face with a little oil on the muzzle and around eyes. Make sure your number is clearly visible to the judge—most competitors affix theirs to the corner of the Navajo saddle blanket. Always dust your boots off and smile—you're supposed to be having fun.

Tip 84. Are we there yet?

It seems a bit obvious, yet it never fails that somewhere, on some show day, a rider misses every class because he's doing battle with his horse while trying to load him in the trailer. The morning of your show is not the time to find out that your well-trained, immaculately groomed show pony is travel-shy. Make sure that your horse is comfortable loading, traveling, unloading, and standing quietly beside a trailer before you pay the show fees. Seek professional help if you don't know how to teach your horse to load and have an experienced driver haul your horse if you have never done it before. Even good travelers balk at loading after they've had a bad ride.

Chapter 7.

Class Tips and
Winning Strategies

This chapter brings you some insights into the nuances of Western pleasure and its judging, as well as helpful advice in and out of the show pen.

Be sure that the judge can see your number plainly. Most competitors affix their numbers to their saddle blankets.

Tip 85. Know the routine.

Be aware of what the judge is seeking. He's looking for the horse that appears to be a pleasure to ride. To be a pleasure to ride, the horse must be broke and quiet, soft and responsive, and willing to go with little restraint. Riders will show their horse at the walk, jog, and lope in both directions, and they may be asked to extend the gaits as well.

Riders may be asked to reverse direction only at the walk or jog, then line up, where the horse will have to stand quietly among the throng of other riders and horses. When the judge asks, the horse needs to back up correctly in a straight line.

A horse displaying good gaits, a beautiful headset, and a pleasant attitude will do well in the class.

Tip 86. Know the nuances of the scorecard.

Horses will be judged on manners, performance, and suitability to give a pleasurable ride. The horse's head should be carried at an angle that is natural and suitable to the horse's conformation at all gaits. He should have a stride of reasonable length in keeping with his conformation. He should have enough cushion to his pastern to give the rider a pleasant, smooth ride. The horse should carry his head in a natural position, not high and overflexed at the poll, nor low with his nose out, or behind the bridle. The horse should be relaxed but alert and ready to respond to the rider's commands without excessive cueing. When asked to extend the jog/jog-trot, the horse should move out with the same smooth way of going.

There is a variety of apparel seen in pleasure classes. One caveat: never let your clothes or equipment be better than you.

Tip 87. Dress for Western pleasure.

While Western pleasure has a definite laundry list of what qualities the horse should epitomize, the rider has plenty of leeway to be creative when it comes to show clothes and tack. Always check with your breed association's requirements, but you are pretty safe wearing a long-sleeved shirt, Western hat, boots, chaps, and jeans (or show pants). How you interpret the rest is totally up to you. But always remember that style is a big thing in Western pleasure, and it's incredibly trendy. Set your own trend only if you have the goods to back it up. And above all remember that it's not a fashion show—you need to have your training in place to win, and no custom chaps or 1000XX hats are going to do that for you. Novice riders should stay away from clothes that exaggerate body movement, like ponytails, long fringe, blousy shirts, and big sleeves.

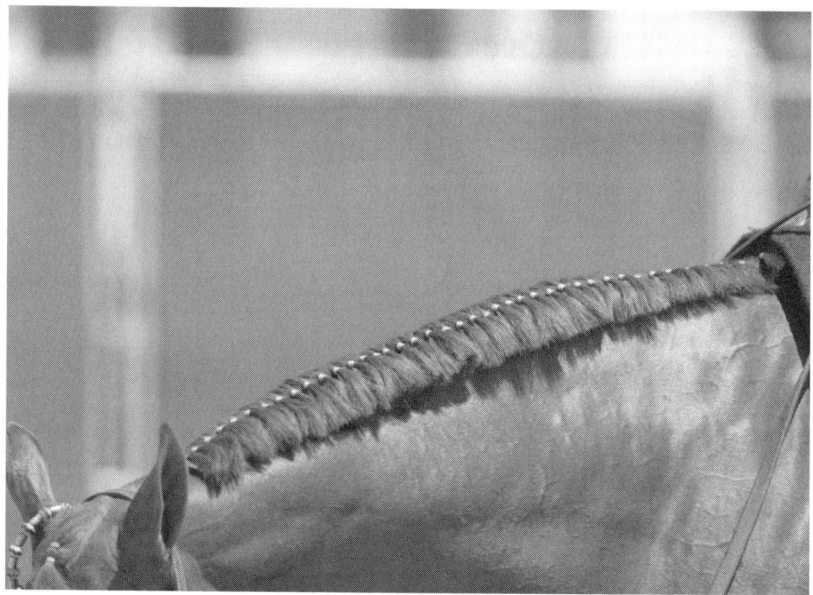

Expert banding needs to take place well in advance. Allow extra time in the wee hours of the morning, or band the night before and use a Lycra hood to protect it.

Tip 88. Your show starts when you get out of bed.

Most show days start plenty early—the curse of the sport. But you can help yourself in the long run by planning ahead. Get to the show grounds with time to relax and warm up your horse properly. If it's a weekend show and your horse will be stabled at the grounds, you'll have a little easier time than if you have to trailer in that morning, but the key is to allow ample time so you don't have to rush and be stressed. If your horse is keyed up, try to longe a little of the edge off. Prep him for your class, grooming and tacking him up. Then warm up under saddle. You should be ready then to face your first class with confidence.

If you have many classes in a row, it's fine to stay on your horse; otherwise, give him a break by dismounting.

Tip 89. Don't use your horse as a sofa.

If you don't have a bunch of classes in a row, get off your horse's back. The only reason you should stay in the saddle is to benefit your horse. Walk him around the grounds to take the edge off, or just take him back to his stall or trailer so he can relax quietly. Your horse is not there to give you a higher viewpoint—he's your compatriot in competition. Treat him as that.

Learn speed control at home so that when you are at the show, you will never be crowding another horse's hindquarters.

Tip 90. Find your place.

When you head into the show pen, enter the arena and find an open spot on the rail. Don't crowd up against the horse in front of you—leave at least two horse lengths between you and the horse in front. Your job is to keep your horse clear of any traffic jams and show him off as best you can. If your horse gets too close to the horse in front, your only option is to move well to the inside without breaking cadence and pass to the next open spot. Passing other horses isn't desirable in pleasure horse classes, but you don't want to break cadence by checking him and shortening up your stride. However, if your horse is continually passing all the other ponies, it looks like he's racing along. You'll have to work on your speed control at home. Use your peripheral vision to always be aware of who is around you and where you need to be. If you're coming up on the horse ahead, go deep into the corners of the arena to gain a little breathing room.

A well-matched pair are a formidable opponent in western pleasure.

Tip 91. It's all about attitude.

A well-trained horse can get you into the show pen, but details and appearances are a huge factor in Western pleasure. The horse and the rider's turnout have to be immaculate in order to be pinned in the class, and horse and rider must show excellent synergy in the class. You can't muscle a pleasure horse in class and expect a ribbon. A horse should be a top mover, but even more so, he should have the right positive, winning attitude. That goes for the rider too. Even though the horse is the one being judged, the rider can still make or break the class.

Tip 92. Common faults that you will be scored down for include:

- Nervous at walk
- Jogging during walk
- Not performing a two-beat jog
- Failing to jog both front and back
- Wrong leads
- Breaking gaits
- Not performing a three-beat lope
- Pulling on the bit
- Hard or rough riding
- Throwing head
- Gaping at the bit
- Constant bumping the bit by rider
- Rider obviously schooling/correcting
- Not backing
- Rearing
- Inconsistent gait

Tip 93. Carefully extend your jog.

If the judge asks for an extended jog, take a few steps of regular jog and then ask the horse to lengthen his stride. If you ask too abruptly, your horse may think you're asking for the lope and break gait. A few jog steps before sending your horse into the extended jog shows the judge that you know how to properly ask and execute the transition into the gait.

Tip 94. Your first impression counts.

In a class, particularly a large one, the judge doesn't have a whole lot of time to spend on each rider. That's why you want to make your first impression count. When the class starts, the judge immediately begins to start placing riders, and he spends the rest of the class trying to confirm that he's right about his placings. So start out strong so that you make that list of top riders, and never stop showing, since a mistake later in the class can bump you down in the ribbons, too.

Tip 95. Some typical mistakes.

Even if you have the best moving horse in the world, you can still be out of the money if you make some common mistakes. To better your chances, avoid making any unnecessary errors. Some of them include carrying your hand too high, not stepping into the requested gait correctly (jogging instead of loping), waiting too long to make direction and gait transitions, and sloppy direction changes.

Use the warm-up ring to do any last-minute schooling. Don't school your horse in the show pen.

Tip 96. Do your schooling outside the ring.

Judges know that riders use the opportunity when he's not looking to correct their horse's headset behind his back. The judge can tell that a correction has taken place because the horse was going a certain way, and when he sees him again, there is something different. Many judges think this is not respectful and that it's like trying to get away with something. Just ride your horse to the best of your ability and keep the jerking, bumping, and pulling on your horse's head out of the ring.

Tip 97. Finesse things you can control.

When the competition is fierce, you can still win by making the most of your horse. Make sure that your transitions are clear and obvious and that your horse doesn't stumble into them. Keep your body language down to an absolute minimum, and maintain excellent body position throughout your ride. When you change direction, make sure you do it promptly, smoothly, and in rhythm with your ride. You have the option of doing a 180-degree pivot or a small circle, but don't stop your horse beforehand.

Tip 98. Slow going.

There is a prevalent attitude in Western pleasure that the slowest horse is the most desirable horse in the class, and so during the class, riders keep their horses going too slow. However, you should always know what your horse's natural cadence is so that you aren't inter-rupting his flow. If you are on a horse with a bigger flowing stride, he probably is going to pass some of the cramped up, artificially slow horses. As long as he is keeping with the requirements of the class, just pass and keep your horse's natural rhythm going.

Whether you get a ribbon or not, use every competitive experience to display your good sportsmanship.

Tip 99. Be a good sport.

Your sportsmanship is important. You should always have a positive attitude in the class, and outside the arena as well. Don't gloat if you win, and take time to congratulate the winners if you don't. A judge can see who the real sportsmen of the class are, and they do take note of it. Any demonstrative sore losers will be mentally noted.

Tip 100. React promptly to the judge's commands.

We've all seen it before. The announcer calls for riders to jog and nothing happens. They are all waiting until the horse in front has begun his transition before they go. Some even wait until they know that the judge is watching them. This annoys a lot of judges. If the rider in front of you isn't going anywhere, ignore what he or she is doing and get it in gear. A few seconds is OK to set your horse up for the transition, but any longer is disrespectful of the judge and his time.

Tip 101. Don't stop showing.

Just because you make a mistake, don't let it get the better of you. You have to keep showing if you want to win. Your mistake might not be as costly as someone else's. The judge will be comparing your ride to the others in the ring. So don't get angry, give up, or become frazzled over an error. Get it out of your mind and instead concentrate on the good things you can do. Say you blow your transition into the lope by adding a few jog steps. Just overcome the negative thoughts and instead concentrate on the fact that your horse does beautiful flowing pivots to reverse direction. Don't beat yourself up; just get your job done. You still might be in line for a ribbon.